Key Strategies *to* Grow Profits, Boost Sales
and Build Trust

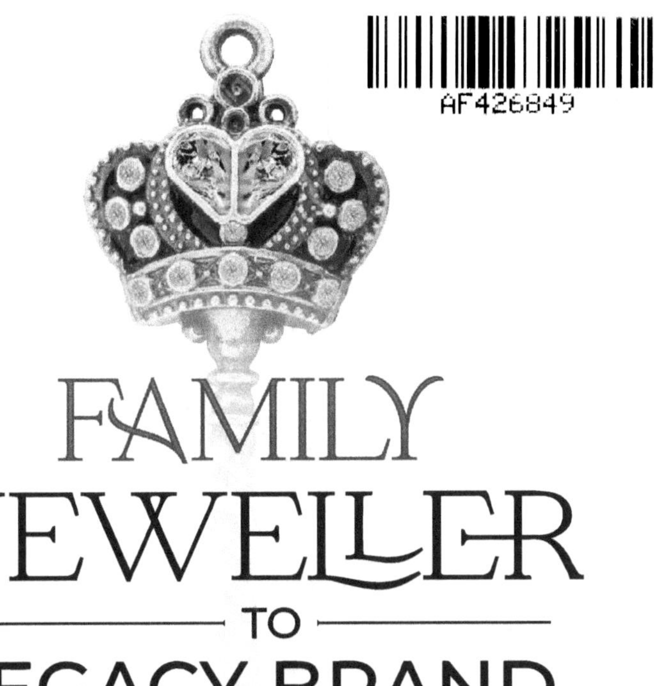

FAMILY JEWELLER
TO
LEGACY BRAND

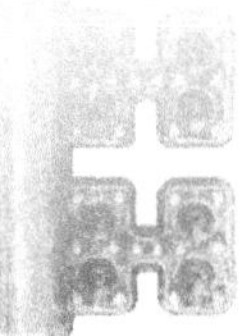

Key Strategies *to* Grow Profits, Boost Sales
and Build Trust

FAMILY JEWELLER TO LEGACY BRAND

SAURABH A. KHANDELWAL

Worldwide Published by
Pendown Press

PENDOWN PRESS LLP
An ISO 9001 & ISO 14001 Certified Co.
Regd. Office 3767A, Kanhaiya Nagar,
Tri Nagar, Delhi-110035
Ph.: 8180886000, 9650072927, 8595249536
E-mail: info@pendownpress.com
Branch Office 1A/2A, 20, Hari Sadan, Ansari Road,
Daryaganj, New Delhi-110002
Ph.: 011-45794768
Website: PendownPress.com

First Edition: 2023

ISBN: 978-93-5554-659-3

*This book is dedicated to
my first gurus my parents
Mrs. Krishna &
Mr. Ashok Khandelwal*

Contents

Foreword

Welcome to the captivating world of high-margin jewellery sales, where the artistry of design meets the skill of persuasion. In this remarkable book, **"Family Jeweller To Legacy Brand,"** you will embark on a transformative journey that unravels the secrets behind successful sales in the dazzling realm of jewellery.

In an industry that thrives on exquisite craftsmanship and timeless beauty, the ability to effectively communicate the value and allure of each precious piece is a skill that sets exceptional jewellers apart. With this book as your guide, you will gain invaluable insights and expert advice on how to navigate the intricate dynamics of the jewellery market and master the art of selling high-margin jewellery.

Drawing upon years of their experience and the wisdom of accomplished industry professionals, this book serves as a beacon of knowledge, illuminating the path to remarkable sales performance. From understanding the psychology of buyers to leveraging the power of storytelling, every chapter is carefully crafted to equip you with the strategies and techniques necessary to thrive in this competitive landscape.

"Family Jeweller To Legacy Brand" goes beyond the surface of salesmanship, delving into the nuances of relationship building, building trust, and creating exceptional customer experiences. It emphasizes the importance of authenticity and integrity in every interaction, reminding us that success lies not just in closing a sale but in nurturing enduring connections with our clientele.

As you embark on this enriching reading experience, prepare to be inspired, challenged, and enlightened. Whether you are a seasoned professional or a budding jewellery entrepreneur, this book will empower you to reach new heights of success in the world of high margin jewellery sales.

I applaud the author for their dedication and commitment to sharing their invaluable expertise, and I extend my sincere gratitude to them for presenting this comprehensive resource to all aspiring jewellers. May this book be your guiding light as you navigate the fascinating realm of high-margin jewellery sales and discover the boundless opportunities that await you.

Wishing you a transformative and prosperous journey!

~Lalit Musal
Motisons Jewellers Jaipur

Preface

In your hands in perhaps the only book dedicated to jewellers. It has been painstakingly developed for over more than 4 years. This book is the first part of series based on research and analysis done by the author Saurabh A.Khandelwal in the past 25 years. He is the first retail jeweller growth specialist in India. What we had to learn through years of hit and trial or experimentation is now presented in this book in most practical manner to be applied immediately with minimum planning and efforts. Through this book you will be able reach your desired results in a much faster and efficient manner. Throughout this book you will find some simple exercises or things designed to walk you through an easy to use approach of applying the concepts covered in different chapters.

Thank you for allowing me to be part of your journey towards growth, success and transformation.

If you have any further questions or enquiry you can directly reach to me:

E-mail: ceo@dhanvidiamond.com

Happy Reading and Implementing.

~SAURABH A. KHANDELWAL

About Author

Saurabh A. Khandelwal, currently the Principal CEO at Dhanvi Diamond, has a rich and illustrious career as a businessperson and an expert gemmologist. His father, Mr Ashok Khandelwal, expanded his father's jewellery business into an actual store, wholesaling silver jewellery, he established the new trademark, "OMJ65" (renowned trademark in Silver Trade Pan India), and kick started the new era of silver purity.

While Saurabh's father ran his jewellery store, Saurabh got a law degree to complement his existing commerce background. Following this, in 1999, he achieved a diploma in Gemmology and Diamond Grading from the prestigious institute IIG and IGI. Armed with such knowledge, he joined his father in 2000, thus marking his foray into the jewellery industry.

In 2001, Saurabh Started his 1st jewellery retail store, "Gehna".

In 2002, he refined his gemmology expertise with a Diamond Grading diploma from the International Gemmological Institute. This enabled him to enter diamond manufacturing and trading in 2003, paving the way for his success in the Diamond supply business. He used his extensive training and abilities to improve the business while finding expert artisans who could match his specialisation. In 2007 he started B2B brand "DHANVI".

In 2020 he established a diamond jewellery manufacturing unit. In 2022 they added another feather in the cap with the launch of their new diamond jewellery Brand "PREMIO" which targeted towards the Office going genre.

Saurabh in his lustrous career of 25 years has brought numerous innovations to all segments of Jewellery industry be it manufacturing, trading or retailing.

Today DHANVI & PREMIO products are available at more than 187 jewellery stores across 50 cities in India.

He managed this while conducting numerous seminars and workshops on financial independence through 2017-18. In 2020, he received his most recent honour as a chief guest at a business summit in Amity University. His achievements can be variedly seen in different news channels and media newspaper and magazines.

His accomplishments as an individual and a leader are well represented in the way he runs Dhanvi Diamond. With such expertise, he manages the company efficiently, ensuring excellence in every project he undertakes not just for his company but for all his associated clients jewellery stores.

His company's Cultural statement stands true towards their ethics and values.

"साथ चलें साथ बढ़ें *V R D Best*"

Who is This Book For ?

- Any Jeweller who owns a Jewellery Showroom or multiple jewellery outlets.

- Any jeweller who is working from home

- Anyone aspiring to open a Jewellery showroom

Though this book has been written keeping in focus Jewellery Retail sector but the fundamentals and psychology discussed here in shall apply to any Retail industry. Since topics discussed in the book will broadly apply to understanding the mindset of a customer and will help in gaining trust and creditability hence resulting in increased customer footfall and increased profits.

Why This Book ?

Before you read any book it is important to understand why and where are you investing your time and what will you achieve after reading this book.

After reading this book, you will be able to-

- Transform yourself into a Brand.

- 5 techniques to enhance your Brand presence.

- Understanding of jewellery customer behavior and psychology.

If implemented with full precision-

- Better control over flow of sales and customers.

- Increase your customer footfall by upto 40% within 6 months.

- Increase your profits by upto 40% within 6 months.

- Transform yourself into a BRAND.

A few exercises have also been incorporated in the book to give a more clarified picture of your present status.

If you complete all these exercises, I can assure you of achieving all your targets of increasing jewellery sales, client foot fall and profits.

I wish you great luck on this journey....

Acknowledgements

Through out the writing of this book, there has been a constant flow of support and motivation.

I would like to thank my wife Neha and kids Dhanvi and Kushagra because it was their time that they sacrificed by letting me complete my research and for writing this book.

Nonetheless my friend Anil Bansal who has given constant guidance and support from the very first day.

To my brother and friend for life Saurabh Tambi for keeping me motivated.

Word of love to all my friends n family for constant support, love and care.

The biggest thanks to all my clients who contributed their valuable feedback so as to make this book possible.

Last not the least my heartfelt gratitude to my various gurus who have given their every bit in making me what I am today, for each one of them has contributed in shaping and polishing my every facet that shines like a DIAMOND.

Thank you everyone who I have not mentioned but they have left their mark in my life.

IMPORTANT STATEMENTS

VISION

To empower 1,00,000 jewellers in India and worldwide and transform them into Organized Jewellery Chain stores.

MISSION

To connect and transform unorganized jewellery sector to be more successful and on a sustainable growth path by implementing TRUST Framework.

GOAL

To Increase customer footfall by 40% and achieve 30% profit growth every year at every jewellery store by simple and effective tactics.

Chapter 1

The Beginning

I come from a very humble background. There's a small village in Rajasthan with the name of 'Harsoli', where my father spent his childhood, later they shifted to Paharganj in Delhi. My grandfather used to deal in bullion but his sudden death shattered everyone's life leaving behind his wife and 3 sons. My father was the eldest and was just 18yrs old studying in B.com at the time of his death.

After his death, there was no financial back up, no one to support. My grandfather must have had this vision of something not being right with him. He left 6 months stock of food ration at home and about 700 rupees. With nobody to support him my father started asking help from relatives, friends for work. Wherever he went seeking for help, no one extended any support or showed any way. He was left with no choice but to start doing odd jobs. For many years he worked as a clerk in Laxmi Commercial Bank and also started doing part time jobs in bullion market. Till he figured it out that a job isn't going to do any better and he needs to start a business to support his mother and 2 younger brothers.

He took some loans, rented a shop and started a small jewellery retail shop.

I saw my father shedding his blood like sweat his entire life, all for a good fortune & future.

It has been 45 years since he has been running his showroom. He got quite successful in all these years, he made homes for us and his brothers, built them their own jewellery businesses.

He has successfully raised his two kids, who are successful in their own independent businesses.

But I don't remember him ever going on long holidays with us. He could not get out of his monotonous routine. Once he leaves his showroom, everything seems to stop working. And still after so many years of experience and time, he is somewhere stuck.

After working hard in all these 45 years and gaining loads of experience, but at the same time his client numbers had fallen drastically post covid and he didn't know exactly what to do next. And over the course of time, he just got himself into a comfortable situation where he doesn't want to get out of this paradox.

It wasn't easy for me either. Living in a joint family, attention & opportunities were very limited. It was always a fight for survival. I only remember the words: not now, we'll see it later, buy it later, we will take this next year and so on.

To earn you need to do lot of tough work and sacrifice, and so I started doing everything and anything without thinking of any pain, time, family or friends & worked tirelessly & selflessly for years.

I started a jewellery supply business from a 30 sq. ft. office in Chandni chowk. The space wasn't even enough to stretch both my hands at my office at the same time. I started Diamond Jewellery supply with very limited inventory of about 25 rings, 10 earrings, 5 pendants and 30 nose- pins. And year after year, I kept growing despite of limited knowledge, various setbacks, no support system and no-one to guide.

I also learnt everything the hard way. Life kept teaching me lessons, I kept learning and applying. I kept sacrificing and kept doing hard work without thinking about anything else but I made sure of one thing that business should keep growing year after year. But as they say, "Learning is a forever process", this process of learning is still on.

Today we have a strong base of clients of about 187++ jewellery stores across India with presence in more than 50 cities and growing everyday. Our presence can be seen across various print media, news channels and other publications.

DHANVI and PREMIO, both are well known B2B Brands.

We are the first company in India to launch TRUST Framework 3.0.

Chapter 2

The Realization

Year 2019 and sudden hit of Covid

Unexpected covid situation came as a big jolt for my business and everyone else's business too. Sales crashed & so did my earnings. Even after 2 years of Covid, I realized that jewellery sales were still not rising while expenses doubled and soon I was in net losses. Instead of earning we were losing money every day. It shocked me to core when one of my jewellery craftsman vanished overnight with my jewellery and it came as a big jolt. To seal my fate all of my clients started delaying payments, the credit cycle started stretching and it all went upside down.

I sat down one fine evening trying to figure out what I was doing wrong. I started talking to my clients and they were also in same situation, their sales were also down, their monthly expenses had doubled and profits were badly hit. But to my despair, I had nothing to answer my questions and to come out of my situation.

It was November and Diwali has just passed when it should have been bumper season for any jeweller but it wasn't, I was sitting with one of my fellow friends who has 2000 square feet jewellery showroom and has been working in this segment for the last 35 years. He has a decent size showroom and decent stock size and client footfall but still his jewellery sales were falling and profits were badly hit, yet he was confident that market would rebound as he was expecting a good marriage season right ahead.

3 Months Passed…

Just last week I was sitting with him again and he was sulking in his thoughts on what is going wrong with his work….He was totally lost in his thoughts with anxiety & confusion was evident on his face.

Well! All of this has become a common fact in last few months. Whenever I talk to any of my client irrespective of location or size, all those family jewellers who have been there in market since 10 or 15 or 35 years were losing turf and that their profits were badly hit and overall sales turnover was down. All our stories were common as most of them were stuck in the same cycle of finance, funding, supplier credit and their business and been shrinking from the past few years.

Not just limited to all this but their customer footfall was also falling. New customer addition had gone down tremendously.

And all of them including me were in a fix.....

Question remained at LARGE.....

How to fix this unprecedented situation?

Where to start and what is the way forward?

Chapter 3

Struck Like Lightning

Q. Whenever I asked anyone why this is happening?

Q. What is happening to jewellery day to day trade or industry?

I got usual answers blaming one or the other reasons for the downfall. Somebody said it is Covid while someone blaming de-monetization, someone said excessive excise duty & GST were the culprits and so on...

I fumbled, was it really Covid or HUID or excise duty strike or de-monetization or something else and suddenly I saw a news - TITAN posting 20% jump in sales in F.Y. 2022 for its jewellery wing - 'Tanishq'.

It struck me like Lightening.

I checked other similar players and the results were astonishing - "Malabar" another leading jewellery chain posted a hefty jump of 35% growth in revenue in F.Y. 2022. and as I got more deeper and unearthed more news, things were astonishing as most of the leading brands story was more or less similar, they all were growing at about or more than 30% every year.

I gasped, trying to understand what is happening.

Questions started flashing in my mind.....

What is that they are doing that they have such growth? Whereas family legacy jewellers are bleeding....

- Is it COVID to blame?

- Is it govt policies to blame?

- What is not working?

- What has shifted in jewellery business?

- Is it HUID or GST?

- Or is it something else?

I was awestruck I had nothing to answer my questions...

Chapter 4

Mind Blown Away

It was not easy for me to digest the facts : increase in profit of all these brands and whenever this thought came across it was like my mind stopped working and my heart started sinking.

I began asking myself questions:

What is happening?

What is shifting in the jewellery market? As I searched for my answers…..

I stumbled upon a report, this report was published on a business standard website and the report was made by HDFC securities (India's No.1 Bank) and it raised the curtains on my mind.

This report clearly mentioned the data of rise of market share of about 15 top brands. When I calculated the figures the results were astonishing. These top 15 brands had grown their market share from 23% to over 42% in last 7 years, which meant every year they increased their market share by about 9% per annum. This was sensational, it wasn't just profits that they had increased but their market share as well.

But how?

ON A TRUSTED PATH
Bifurcation of jewellery markets (%)

Year	Organised*	Unorganised
2016	23.2	76.8
2017	24.3	75.7
2018	29.2	70.8
2019	30.9	69.1
2020	33.0	67.0
2021	35.6	64.4
2022	38.5	61.5
2023	41.7	58.3

Organised players include: Tanishq, PC Jeweller, Tribhovandas Bhimji Zaveri, Thangamayil, GRT, Joyalukkas, Kalyan, Malabar, P N Gad gil & Sons etc. (and eight others)   *Source: HDFC Securities*

And at whose cost?

I sat down and started finding answers to my questions and after days of searching and analyzing tons of data. I arrived at this conclusion that actually it's not just the profits that are badly hit and it's not jewellers that are losing market share but in reality all family/legacy jewellers are them is losing money, making losses and that too about 33 lakhs per year and this is the minimum. It can be even more for a medium or bigger jewellery store.

It is hard to believe.......right. but that's an absolute truth.

Here's a simple exercise for you...... to help you understand this.

Just fill this exercise on the next page and you will get your figure. Just do it by approximation figures, need not to be exact as the result will be nearly same.

Assessment done on basis of Gold & Diamond Jewellery. We are not taking silver jewellery for ease of understanding and calculations.

Exercise 1.1

	Jeweller Reality Exercise (Gold & Diamond)	1 day	1 week (x6 days)	1 Year (x312 days)
A.	Number of Customers Visits/Day:			
B.	Average Sale/Customer: (average sale done to customer for eg. 1 customer bought for 200000, 2nd customer for 50000 and 3rd for 15000 avg will be 88,333)			
C.	Calculate Total Sale (Multiply AxB)			
D.	Sale lost @ 9%			
E.	Average Profit Margin:			
F.	Total Profits Lost:			

Now my friend tell me, how many more years you want to run your Jewellery Showroom.

A. Write number of Years:

B. Write profit lost per year from the exercise

Total loss in X Years (multiply A x B)

***

This is true reality and to my fair knowledge this is a minimum figure and this rate of 9% market share is going to go faster, as the pace of technology, government policies act in favoritism of big players and other factors will double their growth with time.

Chapter 5

The Big Question

WHAT TO DO?
HOW TO DO?

A nd anxiety kept building up, when another research suggested that this growth surely would be in double digit every year.

Now what I am going to tell is not just a fact but the truth: In the 5 years history will be re-written in jewellery sector. Everything is going to change, the way jewellery is sold and purchased. Market and my research says in next 5 years a big transition is underway and organized players market share could reach upto 80% of the Indian markets. It is all at the cost of regional family jeweller, who have suddenly lost that sheen, that edge.

Market is shifting from Un-organized to Organized sector

This was my tipping point, when my blood started rushing to my brain and I felt restlessness all over my body and from here I began to do this research work and started finding answers to my questions.

I started digging deeper into it and finding reasons why this major shift is going on in market.

My research took me to a surprising fact, what is it that these top brands are selling:

- Are they selling Best Designs?

- Are they giving Best Prices?

- Are they giving all the small services as a family jeweller gives?

- Are they personally related to customers as family jewellers?

- Do they have everything under one roof?

- Do they give Instant Cash buyback?

- Do they offer everything under one roof?

Answer to all these questions is a Big No….. But still they are growing.

What do you think is the answer to this question:

Why Brands are growing at such faster pace and taking away the business of small/medium/family jewellers?

Ans.____

____

____

Write your answer and email it to us for a special gift…. Email to – ea@dhanvidiamond.com

Chapter 6

The Start of New Era

I delved deeper and found some interesting facts. All of them are selling at very high costs almost 4 to 5 times than a normal jewellery store. Most of them have one third of the inventory of a medium size jeweller. They are unable to provide 80% of the services or facilities than a family/legacy jeweller could provide.

But fact still remains the same.....

These big chain stores have actually changed the Equation....

These have changed the way jewellery is sold. They have changed the experience of customer when they come to buy jewellery. And change in experience is not just at store but everywhere in the customers eco-system.

- From website to facebook & Instagram to other social media platforms.
- From mobile application to personally engaging campaigns.
- From product information to packaging and educational marketing collaterals.

- From personal attention at stores, managing every small factor to enhancing experience and creating a psychological impact on the customers mindset.

They have managed to earn bigger Trust & Creditability in general customer mindset.

This is how they become a BRAND.

Now it might seem too easy at times creating a website or mobile app or showroom environment in synch or similar to any branded showroom.

But in reality it is a very intrinsic and deep dive job of understanding customer behavior and how everything will interact with client and give a feeler of the BRAND.

And with this power they are able to sell at 2 to 4 times the profit of a normal family jeweller even with half or one-third of inventory.

Just imagine for a cup of coffee how much you are ready to spend. Usually its 20 to 30 rupees but in a normal café it will cost upto 100-150 rupees. And same coffee at Starbucks will cost you about 200-300 rupees.

What is it that Starbucks is selling?

It's not just the Coffee.....

But the Experience of Drinking that Coffee.....

But what do we do about it -

- What to showcase?
- What to display?
- How to create that experience?
- How to educate?
- How to develop effective marketing collaterals?
- How to create interactive ecosystem?

Next 5 chapters will reveal all this and much more.....

I will guide through the process of becoming a Jewellery Brand....and attain High Margin Jewellery Sales.

Let's START! Begin the New Era.....

Chapter 7

Technique 1 Power of Context

Context can be broadly described as the environment through which a customer interacts with us. Context is the first and most important aspect of any shop, showroom, market or business ecosystem.

Broadly Context can be divided into 2 parts:

A. Internal Context

B. External Context

Internal Context

It means everything inside your jewellery store that communicates with the customer. Once a customer enters into your showroom and till he buy or walks out of showroom, during this time period everything is talking to them, communicating to them.

First Impression

Starting from your Guard when he opens the door and the way he greets the customer, the addressing staff, their appearance, their first eye to eye contact with the customer, the way they smile, the way they greet, their dressing sense, everything is making an impression on your customer's mindset.

Apperance

The colour of sitting(sofa), the way jewellery is displayed, the lighting effect, the fragrance in the air, the music around the store, the cleanliness of the place, the placement of each n everything counts.

All these factors become part of the context of your showroom (store).

Showroom Lighting

Right lighting while showcasing the jewellery again plays a crucial role especially in Diamond Jewellery and Gold Jewellery.

Communication

Language preference plays an important part in changing perceptions of your customer and it directly effects the buying behaviour.

Customers are seldom aware of the influence of these environmental contexts on their behaviour but eventually everything counts as you change their mindset by choosing the right contextual settings in your jewellery store.

A real marketer has an opportunity to create customer value by changing these environmental settings through right brand positioning, genuine effective communication, and providing supporting structures.

Optimizing the right interior context will surely enhance your customer experience and in turn your sales and profits.

External Context

External context denotes everything outside your showroom where your customer interacts with your identity. Facia of your showroom, your online presence, your media presence, everywhere or anywhere where your name or presence is there outside the preview of your showroom is your External Context. Recreating and keeping it upto date is as important as the interiors of your showroom. Here are few tips to make your external context factors which make your identity more appealing and make your presence felt.

Front Facia

Did you ever imagine how many people walked outside your showroom in the whole day-time and out of them how many of them stepped inside. The percentage will be less than 1% but those who didn't enter are still our prospects.

First and most important of your showroom external facia. This is the first identity of any showroom. Since this facia is constantly communicating with outside world, it should be best as we all know first impression is the last impression. It is your Trump card of marketing.

Your facia should be designed in such a way that it creates THE PULL factor of people walking, driving outside your showroom.

Re-create you facia, make it interactive and start attracting new clients. Only this action can generate 20% new client footfall. This is one time investment for the next 5 to 7 years.

Digital presence

Second most important aspect of your external context is your digital and social media presence.

Digital presence means:

❖ Your Website

❖ Mobile Application

And Social Media Presence will include:

❖ Facebook Page

❖ Instagram Page

❖ You-tube

❖ Pinterest

❖ Your Whatsapp status

❖ Your Whatsapp Profile & Description

❖ Your Email ID

And everywhere else where you can appear online on internet.

Each of this place should be synchronized and updated on a daily basis. Today's generation is called Mobile generation. Everything and anything is found on internet. When you want anything you just go on google or similar search engine and find related information. Your customers also do the same.

You and your product information should be available online to view and visit. It is then, that you are seen as a brand, as an authority.

Your website should be live and always remember if it is not updated on daily basis then it is as good as dead so you need to have a dedicated team who will update it on daily basis. The same goes for your Facebook and Instagram page and in fact every other social media platform. You can also hire an external agency to make sure your presence is always upto mark n live with new trends as per changing needs and demands of the customer.

When you start building your external context and internal context slowly and steadily your business will definitely transform into a BRAND.

You can simply get next two exercises photocopied or e-mail us to get a pdf link for these exercises and start working on them today.

Upon completing these exercises you will feel great, comfortable, more at ease and tranquil at your workplace/ showroom.

Your customers will have a greater interactive experience to be remembered for a longer period of time.

Do this now…..

Exercise 1.2 : Build My External Context

Target	Create By Date	Managed By Staff/Agency	Frequency
Facebook Page			
Instagram Page			
You-tube Channel			
Pinterest			
Customer Care Phone Number			
Customer Care Email ID			
Live Website			
Business Whatsapp			

These exercises are not inclusive in nature. You can add or subtract other things as per your customers preferences and geographical location.

But by building this contextual environment you are surely going to build your Trust & Creditability and in turn increase your sales and profits to a great extent.

When you control your Context you control your customer's behaviour and in turn their mindset and influence their decision to buy, to a greater extent. Not just this but you start getting recognised as an Organized player and slowly and gradually people will start recognizing your company as a BRAND.

Another exercise for enhancing your Internal Context is on the next page. Similar to previous exercise you can add or subtract multiple things to enhance experience of yourself and your customer.

Exercise 1.3 : Create Internal Context

Target	Implement By Date	Responsible Person	Frequency
Cleanliness			
Guard Greets n Smiles			
Sofa Sitting Comfort			
Staff Dress			
Staff Greet Sense			
Staff Body			
Language			
Sound System			
Aroma/Fragrance			
Organize All Loose items e.g. Pen			
Lighting Effects			
Lights Optimization			
Other			

We have many case studies where we helped our clients create best context and transformed their business to NEW AGE BRAND.

So, just start working and implementing all these things right now.

At the end it will "Rain Profits"

Mantra 1: "Context is the key to success".

Now the time is yours......

Chapter 8

Weapon of Communication

I was visiting one of the jewellery showrooms of my clients Mr. Mahesh Arora though he is more of a friend. He has a nice showroom and a good customer base. After a small discussion I discovered high ticket customers sale has drastically fallen in past few years and also the quality of customers seeking jewellery has also gone down. I can directly relate it to his display style. There was mix use of colors in display trays and necks with no uniformity at all. Theme play was entirely missing. Everything was displayed anywhere. Focus was more on quantity jewellery display rather than quality jewellery display. It was like mayhem all around and in all creating lot of distraction and confusion to the buyer.

This is where things went wrong..........as true as the name of the chapter Weapon of interaction turned to distraction or destruction.

Displaying is an Art and when it comes to jewellery store, right combination of content n products can produce wonderful results.

We seldom focus on displaying anything more than jewellery. Jewellers will spends thousands to lakhs on Jewellery Display trays, boxes etc.. but no one thinks about this:

Q1: What should be the colour of display tray?

Q2: How many products to be displayed in one tray?

Q3: What theme should be used in displaying?

Q4: What should be the colour of packaging and other P.O.S materials?

A general survey of jewellers reveal that Display means displaying of jewellery. And as jewellers, this is where we lost half the battle to Big Brands. Display isn't just about displaying jewellery but also showcasing our culture, our history, our achievements, our unique selling point in a way our customer once entering the store is taken aback by saying 'WOW'… may be they won't say it aloud but we can create the right mindset by displaying the right information.

Displaying is majorly about two parts:

A. The Product Display

B. The Information Display

Product Display

The right Product Display is just not about beautiful display trays or stock boxes or display necks but the right colour combination suited to your geographical location and customer preferences are few of the factors to be taken in mind.

1. Choosing right colour will surely attract customer to buy in a more interactive manner. Jewellery display is a subtle art, so choose wisely when it comes to colours and fabrics.

2. Adding customized display systems to your counter will surely enhance the appearance and look of your showroom.

3. My suggestion is to use light grey or camel brown colour for gold jewellery and Black for displaying Diamond Jewellery. Further, immediately stop using white colour trays and boxes.

4. Every time you should be focussing on **HP Display** or High Profit Display meaning the products that are displayed should have high profit margins.

5. Have a common theme for all your boxes, display trays, display necks and give away packaging boxes and packets.

6. Make sure your products are displayed in synchronized manner and should be rotated in every 7 to 10 days time. Have a sheet made for stock rotation management system and assign any sales staff to have this responsibility of managing the rotation of display articles.

7. Limit the number of articles displayed in tray on counter that means display tray should have ideally 8 to 9 products.

Theme based displa

Display should be a mix match of different products. You should use theme based display on one counter or one area showcasing a particular theme for example if Valentine's day is coming it should have all the heart shaped jewellery, marriage season is coming make one of the counter /section theme based on marriage.

This is a subtle art and you will learn it when you try it, play with it and experiment with it.

Always remember the thumb rule:

"Mantra 2: What you show, will sell".

The nformation Display

Information Display means communicating with the sub-conscious state of customer entering our store.

This display of information will help not only in grabbing attention to our strengths but also in building greater Trust & Creditability in their mindset. Right information display will not just help in building T&C but will also lower down day to day bargaining by our customers.

Here are some ideas for content that could be displayed in a jewellery store:

A. Product information: Highlight the materials used, craftsmanship, gold karatage and unique features of the jewellery.

B. History and cultural significance: Explain the history behind the design and how it is related to a particular culture or tradition.

C. Celebrity endorsement: If any famous person has been seen wearing a particular piece, highlight that fact to attract customers.

D. Gift suggestions: Offer schemes or suggestions for different occasions like weddings, birthdays, anniversaries etc.

E. Customization options: Explain the various customization options available, like engraving or changing the metal type, to personalize the jewellery for customers.

F. Upcoming collections: Preview new and upcoming collections to build excitement and anticipation among customers.

G. Certification: Highlight any certifications or awards the store or its products have received, such as being eco-friendly or conflict-free.

H. Hallmarking & Diamond Certification: These days customers are well aware of the prevailing certifications and hallmarking norms but when displayed it helps in objection handling on auto mode.

I. Other Highlights: This list of things is not exclusive but you can devise your own ideas to showcase.

The motto is that the focus should be on highlighting the quality, uniqueness, and value of the jewellery, along with building a connection with the customers.

These ideas are not limited to only what's written in the book but should be explored variably to your gain your customers bigger trust, confidence & creditability.

You can also showcase your Promise. Build a story around your Name and make sure your every sales person talks about your story. This will help in building a personal connect with the customer and make them more comfortable and open.

When our PREMIO Branding team by using correct display techniques changed the display systems and display information at our partner stores the results were astonishing. Their high ticket client base increased multi- fold and they saw a steep jump of 40% in profits.

Exercise 1.4: Stock Rotation Management System

Counter No.	Last Change On - Date	Next Change On - Date	Staff Responsible
1			
2			
3			
4			
5			

Exercise 1.5: Create 1 poster mentioning the right gold purity and hallmarking names. If you want you can create multiple posters, you can simply use the ideas from the chapter. This exercise is meant to make a rough sketch and then get

this idea of yours to be made professionally by a professional designer and get it printed and pasted at most ideal location in your store.

Create 2nd poster mentioning Diamond 4c's and their grading terminology and norms.

Create 3rd poster showcasing the return, exchange policy offered by us for the customer. And so on…

— Happy Drawing —

Chapter 9

Lost Art Personalization

I was sitting with one of my clients Mr.Robin Gupta, who was disappointed with his customer quality. It was not as great as it had been when he and his father started thirty years back. During this long journey they have created a legacy amongst their customers but suddenly in past 2 years they have lost sheen and touch with their old customers. Now he couldn't find quality customers and also new walk-ins have slowed down drastically. To make matters worse, he realized that high ticket client's sales has gone down by more than 80%. He had asked from some of his clients who recently had marriage in their home that why they didn't buy jewellery from them and they replied they had bought it from the new branded jewellery store. He tried to analyze why that long relationship customer didn't buy from him but from some branded store and this was a clear indicator that there is an issue with trust or creditability factor as customer is perceiving these BRANDS as more credible and trustworthy.

I am not saying that the customer doesn't trust you but these BRANDS have managed to build more trust and creditability and in turn have become a bigger authority in your customer's mind. And all of this was affecting my clients(you), both professionally and personally.

But question comes "What to do?"

I had three long days of brainstorming on how to promote new jewellery collection without spending on advertisements. Everyone believed advertisements are costly and have lost their effectiveness over the years (I too believe so).

The era of mass media marketing is over. It is the age of direct & personalized marketing now… which is what this story is going to reveal - how to use direct, personalized marketing concepts that can increase the possibility of sales and in turn of course profits.

Mantra 3: "Better you know better you can serve" Personalization carries the highest attention…

Personalization basically refers to personal touch of yours with your client that has been there since many years but has lost it's sheen now. I remember for a few months, I used to sit at my uncle's silver wholesale shop, he was quite good at connecting with his clients. He used to talk to them on a very personal note and length. These personal talks cemented his relationship with his clients and in turn resulted in greater Trust and Creditability.

The question arises how to create personalization in today's fast moving world, where attention span is super low and time is a big constraint.

Here are a few tips to nurture this…

Data is Future

The future of the jewellery business in India is expected to grow around personalization. These days every jewellery brand is investing tons of resources and money in data storing, analysis and solutions that are aimed to personalize their communication with their target customer.

For instance, if any customer who has visited the website or searched on web or viewed a certain type of necklace, you can automatically recommend them similar necklaces to personalize their shopping experience. Similarly, if any customer comes to your Jewellery store and purchases any jewellery for example a solitaire ring, you can send them messages or emails that are targeted around this purchase. We can make a message that this exclusive new collection bracelet will create an exceptional style statement when you wear it with the solitaire ring that you purchased recently.

Such a level of personalization assures greater loyalty and recurring business from your customers.

Personalized Services

You can simply invite your client to visit your store for a free check-up of Diamond Jewellery that they purchased any time. You can simply align a staff to regularly call n invite them.

It is important to develop and create brand loyalty. It needs a deep understanding and rigorous follow up system with your customers to keep high level of warmth and attachment with your brand.

It takes years to build up trust n understanding and loyalty but it take continuous efforts to nurture this relationship. Once you start watering this relationship seed, one day it will nurture into a plant and someday into a tree with fruits but the idea is to keep watering, keep feeding this plant, keep nurturing this relationship. And a secret this practice is as good for any relation and with anyone.

Create Touchpoints

Touchpoint means everywhere and by every means creating communication point/channels with your clients. For e.g. acknowledgment of items received or sold, wishing on birthday/ anniversary and so on.....

Touchpoints are very essential to identify or create and make every communication memorable and remarkable. Touchpoints does wonders in driving higher customer retention and building long lasting relationships with customers. The right ingredients of creating effective touchpoints will add wonders to your outlook and perception on your customer's mindset.

Ingredients of creating Touchpoints

- **Clear communication:** your message should be clear n precise and hit directly to the mindset of your customer.

- **Confidence building words:** Usage of phrases or words which tell your experience or create more confidence on your name or branding.

- **Showcasing Care n Love:** Draft such messages which show care and have feeling of love. Usage of such words will help in gaining personal connect.

- Building on Trust: Use or make creatives, slogans, stories which build more trust on your BRAND.

- **Data bank:** Have a system to manage your data efficiently on important days n dates.

- **Follow up system:** A precise follow up system to keep in touch with your client is important for creating a top of the mind recall always when they think of jewellery.

This list is not inclusive you can add more ingredients to this and more you think, more you add to this equation you tree will bear more and more fruits.

Steps to create Touchpoints

- Map every communication already going on with clients.

- Create Databank based on location n age etc..

- Re-design all content of present communication.

- Flow-system of all communications what will go 1st, 2nd and 3rd. Assign clear timelines.

- Assess all possible new communication ways to open interaction channels/mediums.

- Design attractive, interactive content for new communications.

- Mark responsibility of Touchpoints who will overlook and do the process.

- Align staff for using pitch and handling replies.

- Training on what, why and how of communication.

- Periodic Assessment of Touchpoints.

- Follow up is the key to achieve great results in establishing a long term relationship with your customers.

Types of Touchpoint

1. Upselling Touchpoint

For example a ring sold to a client and now you need to create a communication channel for upselling a matching bracelet saying since we remember you bought this ring from us and we just came across that the same matching design bracelet. We would love to share it with you.

2. Remembrance Touchpoint

Happy Birthday Message

Don't just send a message on whats-app but send an offer to buy something this time or give something free.

Similarly on Anniversary send a message avail a free gift coupon of dinner or movie for two on visiting our store.

3. Care Touchpoint

Service System: Service in jewellery? What the heck….. Yes, my friend it is the biggest opportunity or I should say lowest hanging fruit to double your jewellry sales and we all should start immediately.

Create a service program for all clients

Issue voucher stating free service

Now what will we do in service? Here are some ideas for you-

- Free Service Coupon 1 - Check up of prongs in Diamond jewellry
- Free Service Coupon 2 - Check up of screws/joints/ hooks in case of gold and diamond jewellery
- Free Service Coupon 3 - Free one item Polish/ Rhodium service.

Now when you give this booklet, it will do miracles. As per research conducted by our team at various stores where we implemented this idea, it showed 56% of clients turned up at the store to get their jewellry checked up and when they turned up 50% of them bought something new from the store. Isn't it brilliant. It not just helped in increased sales but customer loyalty and of-course profits. Remember to mention validity on coupons. So that a time-bound urge is created to visit and use the coupon.

You see a simple, easy to execute and low priced touchpoint but an excellent way to convert sales.

Build more ideas around this and you will be the winner in the game.

4. Feedback Touchpoint

Feedback is the backbone of client relationship. A happy client will bring 2 more clients but an unhappy customer will tell 20 people about it. Taking feedback is an art and no client should leave the premises without giving the feedback. Make a pre-set feedback form and make sure your sales staff always have them filled up.

Basic Feedback Format:

Name:

Phone No.:

What do they buy?

Why did they buy it?

If they didn't buy, what is the reason?

Feedback:

5. Follow-up Touchpoint

After a client buys a product, giving a simple call to know if everything is fine or they need any assistance or want to buy something else.

Here are some example for creating follow up message system. Make sure you make your own set as per your client needs.

Do you want to keep your jewels safe n secure? Simple tips to keep your jewellery safe:

- Always double check your locks- always ask someone else to check that the lock has been secured or not.

- It you have a stone or diamond ring, always check the prongs, if anyone of them is loose, don't wear that jewellery. Take it to your jeweller to get it repaired.

- Keep a check on wear n tear of hinges, joints, prongs.

For enhanced and thorough check-ups do visit our store regularly.

Such communication will help in increasing belongingness and sense of care amongst our customers.

You can think of such similar things to not only increase your sales but also profits.

When our PREMIO Branding team applied such techniques to our dealer stores the results were mind- boggling with customer retention n repetition increased by upto 40% in just 4 months. Loyalty factor increased multifold at our partner stores when we applied more than 50 touchpoints and applied a full deep driven communication channel of full 1 year.

So, what are you waiting for.....

Pen down you own set of touchpoint.

Exercise 1.6 : Create a flow of communication done with your customer starting from once the customer enters your showroom and till he buys and then second step till he comes back again to buy....

Exercise 1.7: Draft a personalization message and send to 10 clients right now.

Draft another message and align your staff to send it on a future date.

Special Gift: A special gift awaits you.

Draft a personalization message and email to us on ea@dhanvidiamond.com

And the best message will get a surprise gift from the author.

What are you waiting?

Complete the exercise and claim your gift today...... Personalization can do wonders!

Get in touch with all of them right now...your customers are going to love this....

Chapter 10

The Loyalty Engine
Educate Your Client

One day at one of my partner stores we were discussing over some pricing challenges. Suddenly when a customer started arguing over hallmarking and due to incompetent staff knowledge and lack of education of the client and staff resulted in sales drop.

It is important and evident from various such incidences that many a times client questions our integrity. Whatever we are selling to them, they see us as another dealer, vendor, jeweller.

So, what can we do to improve or increase our authority in our customer's mind.

The only way around is to educate your client.

Distribute Knowledge

Bringing more knowledge base information to your customer will automatically make your customers see you as a brand authority.

Creating and sharing such creatives on Whatsapp or your own social media pages or you-tube channel or pictures or material and anything which enhances knowledge base of your customers so that the silent questions that their brains are seeking automatically gets answered and they see you as an authority.

Few examples:

- Send a creative showing relevant hallmarking signs.

- Make a creative on steps to identify HUID mark on Jewellery.

Displaying Relevant Information at store

This is the most effective technique in building Brand Trust. Make informative tent cards, brochures, pamphlets all aiming towards educating your customers and see them acknowledging you as an authority.

Because when you show them the real hidden(behind the scene) picture or information, their Trust on you and your Creditability in their mind will increase multifold.

- Display Hallmark Signs at Store

- Poster showcasing right purity in various Karats

- Display Return/Exchange Policy

Become Digitally advanced

- Buying a Digital Microscope - you can buy this online for as low as Rupees 1990/- a simple gadget, easy to set up, easy to use. Show them right HUID marking or hallmark signs on jewellery live and see the magic in their eyes.

- Buying Karat-o-meter - Tanishq created a multi-billion rupee brand just by this 1 trick showcasing purity of their gold and customers gold. And still we think karat- o-meter is an expensive machine.

- Buy Girdle viewer - In case you need a microscope with in-built screen. It is a flaunting addition to your showroom. Costs around 30,000 rupees but really effective for checking Diamonds n Solitaires.

- Buy Hand-held Light Magnifier - this is the cheapest and easy to use gadget. Costs around Rs. 500-1000.

- Buy or install a new LED which runs in loop videos of general interest on jewellery. And after every loop play your own video showcasing your history.

- Buy Diamond Checker: Show them they are buying real diamond. The sound of that beep on the diamond checker will be proportional to bigger smile on their faces…do observe that.

Create Giveaway Card

- Jewellery is made for generations. When we buy jewellery it passes on to our generations. But this flow of jewellery can only happen when the jewellery is preserved and stored properly.

Example of giveaway Card

Example 1

- ❖ Few points to be kept in mind while wearing Jewellery:

Wearing Tips

- ❖ Apply cosmetics without the jewellery- wear the jewellery after the makeup.

- ❖ Never apply any kind of cream or gel while wearing the jewellery- the harsh chemicals in these products can lead to discoloration.

- ❖ No sticky things like oil etc. should be used while you are wearing your jewellery.

- ❖ No spray or perfume to be applied after wearing the jewellery.

- ❖ Clean the jewellery once in a month.

- ❖ Don't wash dishes or do laundry with your jewellery on- The harsh chemicals in the products used for washing, when come in contact regularly with the jewellery, they can either change its colour or can take-off the finish.

Example 2

How do I Store the jewellery?

- ❖ Use cellophane or zip-lock to store the jewellery.

- ❖ Use silica gel pouches for silver, plain gold or diamond jewellery. Keep one silica gel pouch in one silver jewellery piece. The silica gel pouch will absorb the moisture in the box.

❖ Don't use silica gel with the jewellery which has precious or semi-precious stones in it.

❖ Never store jewellery in velvet boxes use plastic, wooden or metal box instead.

❖ Never use cotton for storing the jewellery.

❖ Pack all products separately- Never store two products together, use separate compartments to avoid them from scratching each other.

❖ You can also send an offer message based on this for eg. We care you - For free storage packets or cellophane do visit our store and get special tailor made packs for you... absolutely free.

And this simple message will bring more client footfall to your jewellery store. And what you are giving away just realize this – Information in turn this is Education.

Devise or train your staff accordingly they should also converse in a way as to educate and give right information and right knowledge.

Once you start educating your customers, they will see you as different from others and as an authority as true to any Brand.

Exercise 1.8: Now you can use these points and create your own give away card.

Mantra 4: "More you Educate,
Greater trust you create".

Chapter 11

Gamechanger Time
To Level Up

It's high time my friends. The jewellery sector is going through a major transition. A big shift is happening. A decision made today will decide our future that we become part of this transition or this change will phase us out. The wave of chain stores and brands will surely wash us away.

If your jewellery business is not increasing but shrinking, then it is sure to get finished up some day. Because whatever shrinks has to come to an end point.

The decision to step up and start working and start playing the game of levelling up your setup, infrastructure and first and foremost your thinking, is the key to achieving desired results.

We will discuss some important points and key areas where you need to focus on. And how you can do things one by one. By following this route you will surely be more aware and more in control of your things....

Let's Start and level up your game.....

Mantra 5: "Time to change league, play bigger game".

Level up your Positioning

Look for acquisitions, look for joint venture with Brands. Look out for trainings, business analysts through which you can actually turn around the work. Even if you are hoping to build your own brand and work all the way up there, you can still learn by such ventures and then level up your game at the right time.

When you join hands with a brand you will learn a lot of things and not inclusive to a few things mentioned here –

- How they do their Brand positioning?
- How they work on Stock Management?
- How they handle staff training and alignment?
- What medium to choose for marketing?
- What message to choose to create the right urge in our customer?
- What type of mass need to be targeted?
- What is the right way of communication?
- What market collaterals do they use?
- How to design right information and place them right?

And much beyond that….. Branding is a scientific way of building up things as to the current market requirements and involves deep research and analysis. Well you can spend years doing this but as a jeweller I know you don't have much time to do so much R&D so this is the best way to do it.

JOIN HANDS…..

Staff Training & Alignment

Level up your staff by training and aligning them with your own company growth. It is important that people run the company. They make it or break it. If you don't have right set of people around you they will not grow and they will also not let you grow.

- Build a robust training program for your staff
- Align them with values and ethics of our company
- Align them with the Goal n Vision of the company.
- Ask them to make their own Vision n Goal of their lives.
- Show them the path of their growth and success.
- Plan a hierarchy level and how each one of them can level up.
- Plan and define their roles and responsibility for each staff.
- Have alignment meetings with key staff and guide them with your experience.

These are a few things that you can do to align and build up your staff. Our workforce is the most important part of our engine. Without right combination and alignment, the engine will not work. Because they are the people who will work and get things implemented and get results.

Remember staff is the key to your ultimate success.

Exercise 1.9

❖ Create series of training for Gold jewellery calculation.

❖ Create series of training for Diamond jewellery calculation.

Systems

When you are surrounded by right people, you need to have right systems around you through which everyone in your staff can improve, track and analyze their efficiency.

Level up with automation. Use softwares, excel power to enhance your business capabilities.

With the help of these systems you will slowly and gradually ride up the ladder of building yourself.. And much more... List of Important must have systems:

- Stock Analysis System - what's selling, what to buy and what not to buy?

- Staff Performance System - who is performing and who is not?

- Live website and live stock available on internet with complete jewellery range.

- Social Media - Make your Facebook and Instagram pages live and updated.

- Whatsapp - Get your status updated regularly and upgrade to business version.

- Regular Marketing System – where in you constantly stay in touch with your customers.

There is an endless list to number of systems required to grow but my suggestion is to implement one by one and implement only the required ones.

You can build upon more systems as per your requirement and level.

With right set of people and systems you will become UNSTOPPABLE.

Data Mastery

Data management is the biggest mine that holds the key to your success.

You need to have mastery in data management of your customers and products. The appeal, photography, detailing, professional product photoshoots, professional model photoshoot all become necessary ingredients of managing product databank. This product databank should be readily available with complete details with your team. You need to become master in managing the data be it anything.

Maintaining the right data is an art. Manage data effectively through any CRM available in markets. There are pretty good softwares available in the market to manage your customers data. Beware of data theft as there are many tout software out there.

You can simply manage this data on excel files but remember to keep them on cloud.

Exercise 1.10 : Create Data Sample File

Name	
Tel No.	
Mobile No.	
Address	
Birthday	
Anniversary	
Location	
Remark	

Ask your staff to start writing or storing in an excel file from today.

Exercise 1.11: Create Data Bank On Excel Sheet

It's all about how you can separate yourself from the crowd, all of this will ensure, that you create an edge in the market, you will be able to generate high margin jewellery sales within next 3-6 months.

Wow.... I believe all of this is truly remarkable. What do you think?

Of course this is a time taking, painstaking job to do but the results and outcome is very BIG.

And the time is right to set the field right and start playing the GAME.

Do small things take small steps at a time. Do not start it all together.

Remember 1 step everyday = 365 steps ahead of today. Just take 1 chapter and start executing ....

Chapter 12

Rewind The Learning

Let's do a quick recap….. what we have learnt throughout the book till here.

Anyone can become a Brand. There is a process which you need to follow. Yet it's a slow and gradual process and cannot be achieved overnight but with constant execution and progressive implementation of techniques mentioned in book, that will guarantee the desired outcome.

The author majorly talks about 5 things and if you can change these 5 things then you can double the acceleration and halve the time that you will take to reach your goal.

So let's do a quick recap of what we have achieved till now.

The author shares his life journey of how he and his father struggled in the initial years and then he sets his course on a different unknown path to discover the true secrets behind any successful jeweller. He also highlighted how a jeweller is still struggling with day to day chores, no growth, ever decreasing margins and falling customer footfall. It is important that you take self assessment exercise 1.1 in chapter 4, as what is actually happening out there.

But the BIG question is what is to be done about this situation? And how to go about it?

The reality is that top 15 names in jewellery industry are growing their market share at about 9% CAGR and all this is at the cost of the local jeweller or family jeweller.

The author talks about 5 basic changes that every jeweller should apply so as to start gaining advantage over the current situation.

Let's quickly discuss all of these.

- Change the context of your showroom, by context we mean the environment. Optimizing the right environment will help you gain more creditability of your customer.

  Mantra : "Context is the key to success".

- Choose the right display be it any product display or information display. When you do it right the customer gets more ideas and reasons to buy.

  Mantra : "What you show, will sell".

  Build a system around what is to be displayed and how to be displayed.

- Be on top of the mind of your customer. Have a constant touchpoint system with your customer, keep interacting keep reminding him about you and your products and services.

Mantra : "Personalization carries the highest attention".

Make a strategy around developing effective communication with your customer.

- Educating your client will tremendously help in gaining trust of your client to a greater level. Start showing or giving relevant information to your clients. Focus on bringing more transparency to your customers point of view and see the magic.

Mantra : "More you educate, greater trust you create".

- Level up your game by proper brand positioning, effective stock management, effective data handling, choosing the right message and right mode of communication, build a robust staff training program and most importantly become a brand.

Mantra : "Time to play a bigger game".

These are some important takeaways or key highlights discussed so far in the book. I emphasize on implementing all of these immediately to get faster results.

Remember:

"Execution is the key"

So what do you think about all this…

Chapter 13

It's a Matter of Choice

It is now or never… people say destiny is already written but I believe the decision in a particular moment that you will take will decide the outcome and hence results and finally what we call destiny… We write our own destiny by taking the right decision at the right time.

NOW

You have 2 Choices

Choice 1: Keep working the way you have been as you are doing for so many years with frustration, stress, anxiety, firefighting and fear.

OR

Choice 2: Ensure the success by building robust processes and system and teams to deliver the life of fun, joy, happiness and enjoyment.

What choice you will take?

If its Choice no.1 then this book ends here Or

OR

If you choose to pick Choice no.2 then you have something really special and a unique opportunity is coming ahead.

First, make a choice and write down:

I choose: _________________________________

If its Choice 1 than you can simply proceed to final chapter of the book : The Conclusion and it's over.

But,

If its **Choice No. 2** then you should continue to read the book and proceed with next level of execution and restructure your work with us to live life of your dreams.

If you are on this page, that means you have taken Choice no.2.

Welcome to the world, full of opportunities.

First of all, I want to congratulate you for coming to this section of the book. Because making the choice to work on your future and transform yourself and your business to adapt to new era is no easy decision. This requires a lot of work and attention and guts and of course commitment to self.

Now when you know all the secrets that have been written in the book relating to be successful in jewellery business.

But, given your current scenario of schedule, untrained staff and the biggest factor of lack of time to do EXECUTION.

The final question arises:

How to do it?

and

Where to start from?

I would like you to introduce you to Trust Framework - 3.0

This framework has been built around jewellery business especially for retail jewellery stores. This framework will help you get to your goals faster and in a more effective way, wherein you spend minimum or zero time researching or developing systems and things because we do this for you in the most customized scientific manner. And you only spend time on EXECUTION and focus only on Results.

Trust framework will help you in achieving -

- Upto 50% in customer footfall in the first 6 months.

- Increase in profits by upto 100% within 1 year.

- Build robust system around customer management.

- Build insightful data system on your stock management.

- Re-create you r complete work environment from Logo to website, mobile application to online social media presence.

- Your staff training module and other staff related systems.

- And much more since this is just a beginning…..

In all adding up to transform you into a

BRAND

Now……................Who loves GIFTS?

Write …………………......…...............

(your name if you love gift)

To build this understanding on a deeper level around all of this, you can schedule an **online** one hour "DISCOVERY" session with the author himself to gain better clarity over the subject.

We will build up better clarity on the subject and we will discuss your challenges and set up a customized solution for the same.

Though the value given in this session is itself more than lakhs but as a gesture, this session is offered for just Rs.4990/- ….

So hurry now and register…….**NOW**

It's time for the **Jackpot…**

As I said I want to give you a special gift…

As a valued reader we would like to give you this special offer for this session, in only Rs.99/-

Yes, you read it right full 60 minutes session with the author himself for just Rs.99/-. This is one in a lifetime opportunity.

Don't wait just register now...

Registration link on next page.

You can simply scan the QR Code and fill up the form to register. And we will set up a convenient day and time for you to meet the author.

Scan this...

Don't miss this once in a lifetime opportunity of one-to-one session as those who have attended have got worth greater than lakhs.

Let us begin this life changing journey towards growth and success of your business and make your life full of joy n happiness n enjoyment.

Conclusion

It is apparent that Jewellery retail industry is going through a big transition from Unorganized to Organized way of working. Even the government policies are headed towards the same. The excise duty in 2016, de-monetization in 2016, mandatory HUID norm in 2021 and other similar norms and rules imposed on jewellery sector in the past few years are favoring the organized players. So, its high time that we jewellers need to get in line with these norms and standards and start adopting the organized way of working.

And of course future lies here in our one decision that we have come here to make a mark and this one decision will carry forward our business to our coming generations for a long time.

At the end I want to thank you from the core of my heart. This book is not a theory but a practical approach that I have lived myself and achieved big results. Now it is your turn.....

Happy Jewellinggggggggg.....

With Love

Saurabh A. Khandelwal

Meet SK

A self starter, a learner, a strategist, a dreamer and a gamechanger, a jeweller.

I believe focus is the only weapon for any businessman to get success in any domain but focus need to be a guided focus because only right direction will determine right n fruitful results.

My company manufactures Diamond & Gold Jewellery and provides efficient jeweller management services to jewellers under two premier names of DHANVI and PREMIO.

I believe any one can become a success, the only magic you need is "Focus on One Thing".

I am super rich—enjoy life—spread happiness—love—leave a legacy to be remembered by generations.

My aim is to make a positive difference in the lives of those who are willing to excel and leave their mark.

Swimming—Scuba—Rifle Shooting—Travel are my hobbies.

THE T. R. U. S. T. Framework

Trust Framework is the key to 3X exponential growth of our jewellery business.

We have built TRUST to give a practical edge to our jeweller community.

T. Trends - Ways to Analyze the Quality & Design Trends.

R. Relationship - Steps to build up Relationship with clients.

U. User-centric - Building a user centric stock and lowering your capex.

S. Skillset - Fostering ways to train our staff to handle technicalities.

T. Transform - Internal and External transformation of your showroom.

To know more about T.R.U.S.T. Framework,
get in touch with us today
care@dhanvidiamond.com

The "A" Factor of Life

I always focus, always aim for "A" class in my Life because I believe what you focus on will expand…..

- A class Focus
- A class Peers
- A class Goals
- A class Dreams
- A class Purpose
- A class Individual
- A class Leader
- A class Organization
- A class Vision
- A class Education
- A class Achievements
- A class Numbers
- A class Understanding
- A class Joy
- A class Abundance
- A class Friends

- A class Company

- A class Success

- A class **EVERYTHING**

At the end…..

Stay A class in your life and never settle for anything lesser… God Bless You.

Thank you!!!